BOOKS BY JOHN HOLLANDER

POETRY

Tales Told of the Fathers   *1975*
The Head of the Bed   *1974*
The Night Mirror   *1971*
Types of Shape   *1969*
Visions From the Ramble   *1965*
Movie-Going   *1962*
A Crackling of Thorns   *1958*

CRITICISM

The Untuning of the Sky   *1961*
IDEAS OF MUSIC IN ENGLISH POETRY 1500–1700

FOR CHILDREN

The Immense Parade on Supererogation Day
and What Happened To It   *1972*
The Quest of the Gole   *1966*

TALES TOLD OF THE FATHERS

TALES TOLD OF
THE FATHERS

POEMS BY

JOHN HOLLANDER

ATHENEUM NEW YORK

1975

ACKNOWLEDGMENTS   These poems first appeared, sometimes in slightly different form and with different titles, in a number of periodicals:

POETRY: *The Pictures; A Cup of Tremblings; The Same Question; Glimpses of the Birds; Breadth. Circle. Desert. Monarch. Month. Wisdom; Mount Blank; Remembering the Fountain; After Callimachus; The Hidden Ones; Leaving Delos; A Description of the Celebrated Statue of the Storyteller at Ioannapolis.*

HARPER'S MAGAZINE: *The Moment; The Sign; The Garden; Cohen on the Telephone; The Ziz; Eine Kleine Nachtmusik; Officer's Quarters; The Problem of Pain.*

THE NEW YORKER: *The Shades; Kleines Märchen.*

MIDSTREAM: *The Memento; The Question of Hats.*

THE GEORGIA REVIEW: *Something about It.*

HUDSON REVIEW: *The Muse in the Monkey Tower.*

THE TIMES LITERARY SUPPLEMENT: *Kranich and Bach.*

COLUMBIA FORUM: *Artesian Well.*

THE NEW REPUBLIC: *Given with a Gold Chain.*

CIMARRON REVIEW: *A Quick Dip in the Darkening Pond.*

FOUR QUARTETS (Issue in Honor of Robert Penn Warren): *Rotation of Crops.*

AMERICAN REVIEW: *Burning Leaves.*

OPEN PLACES: *A Late Harvest; A Minor Late Alexandrian.*

UNDINE: *At the Twelfth Hour.*

Examples originally appeared in a Festschrift for I. A. Richards, edited by Reuben Brower, Helen Vendler and myself, and published by Oxford University Press.

Under Aquarius was written for a commemorative volume for W. H. Auden's sixty-fifth birthday, edited by Peter H. Salus and Paul B. Taylor, and published in a limited edition by Random House.

The Head of the Bed was first published in the Poetry Chapbook Series of David R. Godine.

Published simultaneously in Canada by McClelland and Stewart Ltd.
Manufactured in the United States of America by
The Murray Printing Company, Forge Village, Massachusetts
Designed by Harry Ford
First Edition

FOR RICHARD POIRIER

CONTENTS

PART ONE

PART ONE

BEING ALONE IN THE FIELD

What had I fallen to? Even the field
Felt higher than I, the ghosts of its oats
Waving invisibly in the purple
Air above me and the height of my eye.

The sight of my eye lowered toward rising
Ground, the light of my sigh sown there, the cry
Of blood rising toward the spirits of wheat
Rusting their high ears, the listening dew

——All had composed themselves in the field, where
The darker air had flown and alighted,
And there was no light by which I might read
The field, much less as I had always done

Make it out through the Book of the Fair Field,
Or some such book. There was surely no light
For that. The absorbing bare field alone
Lay open like a blind eye turned upward.

I lay flat thus against the horizon
Which drew in towards the ground, as the flat night
Prepared in all directions save for that
Of height its draped, illegible deathbed.

TALES TOLD OF THE FATHERS

I

THE MOMENT

In a cold glade sacred to nothing
He stood waiting, withholding his gaze
From unquestioned sky, unanswering
Grass, he later supposed, all the while
Growing unfelt beneath his bared soles.
The sky was not green although the grass
Was gray, and he felt the moment pass,
With no breath, when some ten of them might
Have come whispering through the dark brush,
Past spaces of water and beyond
Regions of erased shapes in the air,
To conduct him far away on foot
To a place not of earth, but only
Of abominations: dirt and soil,
Shit and mud mingling in wet trenches,
Where he would have stood bound and retching,
Aghast, but of course unsurprised as
Soundlessly the things were done, as then
The trembling foal dropped into a vat
Of rotten wine, the kid fell forward
Into the seething milk—but the wind
Breathed for him; the moment came and went
For the thin ten that time. He would wait.

THE PICTURES

His reflection in water said:
The father is light's general,
The son is but a morning star
Whose very rising into the
Failure of daylight makes the great
Case of upward fall—O see him
Bleaching out in the high morning!

His cold shadow on the rock said:
Under me, unshading, lies the
Skeleton of an Indian.
The dead. The dead are not even
Things. Nor odd beings. Stones and bones
Fall away to bone and stone then
To crumbling, then to part of night.

A CUP OF TREMBLINGS

Facing deep wine raised in the
Tilted, earthen cup, the dark
Opening into further
Dark, eyes wide, he could perceive,
Around the rim of the dark,
Breathings of the afternoon;
As, eyes shuttered, he could see
Sleep, so, opened, they would show
Him death—but now momently
In the heart of the wine, far
Away, the muses of waltz
Moved, as if seen from a height
Down a narrowing defile,
In an unshadowed meadow.

4

THE SIGN

When he saw a skull floating
On the face of the waters
With a mind of air and eyes
Of wind, it was not a sign
Of drowning generations
Themselves now drowned. It was no
Mere wonder of mirroring,
But part of the garbage of
Pain, the usual offal
Of encounter: a fallen
Top of something no choiring
Winds' melismata question,
The dark, hollow shard of a
Vessel of decreated
Clay, a cup of life emptied.

—And seeing it just at noon,
Bobbing on bright water at
The most transparent time, when
He could look back over his
Shoulder and see a clear field,
When his long, ever-vengeful
Shadow vanishes and stops,
For a moment, following:
This was most dreadful of all.

THE GARDEN

High on his brick cliff his garden hung
Open eastward and backed against the
Heights that hid the broad, showy deathbed
Of the sun, whose Tiepolo gestures
He read raving reviews of in the
Fiery mirrors of the west-watching
Windows set in other distant cliffs.
It was there that he muttered about
His pots of spiky dill and broad mint,
His borders of concealing privet.
Edenist of the mid-air, he gazed
At the black oily kernels of dust
Flung as if by some high sower and
Languidly fallen through the forenoon
Over the walls, mingling with his soil.
He had had to make do among smut
And fruitless grit; had lopped and pruned all
The branches of shadow and with care
Hung the leathern mock-adder among
His greens to scare grumbling doves away.
In the evening cool his dull cigar
Breathed and glowed. This was all that there was
To keep. And there was nothing to lose.

THE MEMENTO

Presumably, this is a beach:
Sand, date-colored in the lowered
Shade of the high dunes behind you,
Runs out toward a ridge still sunlit,
Still pale. Dropped below it a few
Feet, more date-color but now wet
Rolls out toward what you can hear as
Water, and what some opening
Door into an adjacent dream
Would show to be sea. Beach, then; but
Why are you here now with the brown
Paper bag unopened before
You? It is almost the color
Of remembered sand. Has it been
Retained, perhaps, for whatever
Is within? I think not, for it
May in fact not be practical—
A dummy bag, that cannot be
Said even to be empty. Still,
It is all you have and all you
Know you have, bent over it but
Staring down the long beach toward where
Mistiness obscures the shoulders
Of the dunes, making a kind of
Horizon out of that meeting
Of what can and cannot be seen.
The paper bag. You will wake to
Bright day with even less than that.

THE SAME QUESTION

I

ONE CREATURE TO BEAR THE WHOLE OF IT?

It is all here. It is all with us:
Pools of water—well, we have our eyes.
Mountains—well, a man is most human
Standing up. Broad meadows—well, we sleep.
Rivers—we do run on, but can come
To join another. Oceans—we can
Remember mothers of our mothers.
Forests—we wander darkly in some
Bright plaza of another; but night
Falls. Sands—seconds of arc in the sets
Of circles nested between our eye
And the rhyming horizon. Deluge—
The first tear of sweat our terror weeps.
Landslide—hear the pestle of thighbone
Grinding away its mortar socket.

ONE GREAT PLATE UPON WHICH EVERYTHING IS ETCHED?

The smaller ones could not bear on their faces
All that variety; strong waters could not
Bite there the wonderful rhythms of the crust—
Salt coasts and fresh, jagged hills and smoothly
Older ones—and all the scratching hand could see
In its unformed dark ground stretched beyond the plate,
The table, the room, fled out the bright window,
Overspilling the cobbled streets of the old
Town, ran over the river into the new,
Beyond the manufacturies of parts and
On into the rising backlands, then off the
Map. And had there not conveniently been
Supplied the Whole Thing, we should have been left with
Bringing in the Catch, Gargoyle, View of the Backs,
The Artist's Mother, Neuschwanstein, The Two Gates,
A trial proof of *Childhood, Summer Evening*
And all the rest, discreetly matted and framed
But unsigned, or if so then of no great price.

COHEN ON THE TELEPHONE

Hello? Something wrong again? O hell!
—Rather darkness audible, abuzz
With nasty wings small enough to whirr
Electrically in a forest
Of noises through which no darkling bird
Squawks its response to darkness, or shrills
Its orisons toward the edge of light.
No lost or dropped angels wander here:
The ghosts of noise are only of noise.

Telephones? Well, a sage said, *they can*
Teach that what we say Here is heard There.
But, grinding away at homely bells,
We can no longer talk to Central;
The Exchanges are unmanned; the poles
Are blown down; your three minutes are up.

Instruments? They are deaf: yea, the sweet
Harp of the psalmist could never hear
Its own early arpeggios rising.
The distant ringing is not the sound
Of another's bell reduced to dry
Gasps: it is produced against your ear.
It is not Levi on the Muzak,
Fiddling tonelessly with the bright dials.
It is Ben Cole, the son of your voice,
Questioning along the deep cables,
Sad and nasal even in his yeas.

And once connected to chaos, then
What engulfs you is the babbling of
The multitude of your descendants
Who clamor for a hearing now, not

Then, begetting echoes of themselves
Even as they swarm in the light wind
That blows among jungles of wiring:
Come, come they sang, but *Abbadabba*
Now they sing; until, as if you heard
The planet's end, they are clicked away.
No dial-tone, like a patient front door
May yet open on fields of people,
Bright fields. There is no waiting for dark,
Nor will the long silence break with light.
But from near, from far, unechoing
In the black sea shell you, landsman, hold
Close against your ear, it comes, it comes:

The next voice you hear will be your own.

THE ZIZ

What is the Ziz?
      It is not quite
Written how at the Beginning,
Along with the Behemoth of
Earth and the deep Leviathan,
A third was set forth (as if air
Could share a viceroy with fire,
A third only): This is the Ziz.

The Rabbi   Can we thrall him and his entailed
Aquila then   Space in our glance? And can we cast
asked: A look wide enough to draw up
A glimpse of fluttering over
The chimney-stacks, of flashing in
Huge fir-boughs, or among high crags
Sinking at dusk? How could we have
Lime or twigs or patience enough
To snare the Ziz? The Phoenix lives
Blessedly in belts of hidden
Fire, guarding us from the hurt of
Light beyond sunlight: but where is
The Ziz? A gleaming, transparent
Class, kingdom of all the winged?
Pre-existing its instances,
It covers them, it covers us
With no shadow that we can see:
But the dark of its wings tinges
What flutters in the shadows' heart.

Even more,   In their last whispered syllables
Rabbi Jonah   The muffled whatziz, the shrouded
said: Whooziz (trailing a sorrowful
Feather from beneath its cloak) tell

False tales of the Ziz: his is not
Theirs, nor he their wintry answer.
—Nor should we desire August light,
Showing a prematurely full
Sight of the Ziz entire, lest we
See and see and see our eyes out:
No: Praised be the cool, textual
Hearsay by which we beware the
Unvarying stare of the Ziz
In whose gaze curiosity
Rusts, and all quests are suspended.

At which
Ben-Tarnegol
recalled:

One day at the end of days, the
General Grand Collation will
Feature the deliciously
Prepared Ziz, fragrant far beyond
Spiciness, dazzling far beyond
The poor, bland sweetness of our meals;
Faster than feasting, eternal
Past the range of our enoughness:
So, promised in time, the future
Repast; but now, only vastness
We are blind to, a birdhood
To cover the head of the sky.

EINE KLEINE NACHTMUSIK

It is when he can barely hear
His own windy shibboleth in
The quibbles of the pillowcase,
The hoarse echo in the cave mouth—
Weighing a weight of fire, or
Measuring a measure of wind—
A roar flickers within. Outside,
The uncomfortable night of
Nothing: the nothing that breath is,
The word of hushed designatum
Insisted endlessly upon
As if one waved at Doctors of
Air, again and again, an ear
Of corn, or drew the hieroglyph
For *stream in flood* as a comma
In a list of necessaries,
And then again and then again.
Doctrinaire of huffa-puffa,
Madman of the emptied shell whose
Creature of meaning dried and died,
He scoops up wind in it, rushing
Out with wordfuls of dead echo
Into the sucking breathlessness,
The wind not pausing to listen.

AT THE TWELFTH HOUR

We who are yet awake
Have forgotten light
We   can   only
Feel what we
Are a-
Mid:
Night, you
Turn a dark
Back upon dreams
Of light remembered
Wearily braving dawn

GIVEN WITH A GOLD CHAIN

Clasping, yet unchained
To what it holds, a hand
Giving of gold may take
Thereby yet something golden.
Chains of iron enforce
Dark bondages, then may break;
Silver dims and wanes;
Brass is brass of course;
And though there was only one
Golden chain once, upon
Which everything depended,
Yours, this common one, bright
But somehow humanely reddened,
Its links remaining right,
Is finite but unended:
Too narrow, like all our circles,
To seem an eternal one,
A serious, fallen chain
Like one of shells or berries
Hung in the gentle arc
Of homely catenaries
Our bodies make—not stark
Parabolas of pain—
When crumpled out of shape
And fallen out of glitter
Into a handful of gold
Chinkingly, will mutter
Still of its olden meaning:
"*Ever is my end
Consumed in my beginning*"
Nothing can ascend
A frail, ungraded chain
Looped, or bunched however,

No Dark Form undertake
To give it an adverse shake
In certainty or doubt.
As you rush into the year
Of life I hurtle out of
I hand you, without fear
That nothing can be maintained,
Gold, like the touch of hands
Clasping, but unchained.

GLIMPSES OF THE BIRDS

Seen over the Fields of Cloud

Ringed with a rainbow,
His plane's shadow far below:
This was vouchsafed him.

Flying into the Unfelt

Huddled in silver
Pinions of his steel eagle,
He drops not down, but
Plummets forward into clouds,
Heavy, level, welcoming.

Blue at Thirty Thousand Feet

High in the world's head,
Reason and rage curve away
In one distant rim.

Simile of the Airplane

As when a sun-struck
Gleam high above the lake's blue
Hangs, and then darkens
Into a fleck vanishing
In the graininess of sight . . .

A Bright Light Shines in the West

Evening star so soon?
No. Low in the March sunset,
Turning, a jet lands.

Layers of the Elements

In the grey pools spilt
From cartons along the ground
Reflected swallows
Skim the pale air. Beneath the
Dead milk, a dark motherhood.

Hieroglyphic Before Dark

With his cold candle
He peered through the blind, amazed:
A burning sparrow
Perched on the gray window ledge
Warming something at year end.

The Flight of the Diary

Pages fluttering,
His decomposition book
Alighted in mud.

Hieroglyphic Just at Dark

A bird of the earth
Perches on a motionless
Shadow of dark branch
Along the ground which is the
Fallen shadow of the sky.

Lines of Type Appear to Move

Swallows darkening
The bright page of day—his poem
Hung on the far wall,

Weeping, the poor auspex reads
The little given to him.

By the Night Shore of a Lake

I have put my thought
Into the talkative waves
Like a resting bird.
Lights dance in the dark water:
My love's on another shore.

Hieroglyphic After Dark

The screech-owl's shriek stabs
My unseeing, not a cry
Of pain, but of night.

A QUICK DIP IN THE DARKENING POND

Angular incidents return from silver mirrorings
Unbent, but this green pond of glass fractures the watery
Idea of my body treading in hung streams below:
The ghosts of floating steadily and slowly glimmer through
Weedier cold layers yet, where green knees, dreaming of mine
Awaken to a dark splash: imprint of corpse in water,
Shadow of clay on air—both yield up their dissolutions.
Only the gleaming mind kicks, in its element of green
Surface aflutter, and refractures broken images.
Silver flashes. Ahead, the crawl snoring forward, bubbled
Air through false thoughts of water above darkness of deeper,
Barely-troubled water. Under that, the dark mud unstirred.

ARTESIAN WELL

for A. R. Ammons

The cost per foot
Is high: to drill
Through clayey soil
With firm pressure
But then to hit
Splintering rock
Of glint, and, less
Resistant, the
Sombre patches,
Shadows of blood.
The deeper, the
Louder the purr
Of wild waters
Coursing beneath
Rock, from distant
Confluences;
The deeper, the
Louder the rock
Roars for a mouth,
All the water
Audible here
Only, below
Where sounds of stone
Occur. Purring
Water is there
Below. We know
We hear water:
Through a tall hole
Bored in water,
Water would eye,
Upward through rock

And skyey clay,
An eye mirrored
In the soiled cloud,
The grayer air.

BREADTH. CIRCLE. DESERT. MONARCH.

MONTH. WISDOM *(for which there are no rhymes)*

Not as *height* rises into lightness
Nor as *length* strengthens—say, the accepting eye
Calmed by a longing of shoreline—
Breadth wields its increase over nothing, to the greater
Glory of nothing: our unwanted dimension,
Yet necessary.

What the *square* can share of its rightness
Extends a just plainness; the sure swerve of a
Curve continues beyond itself.
But O, the old closure! *Circle* of will returning
Inward to prison, wrenching all tangencies back,
Lest there be friendship

Even in clever touchings that the
City solders with pity or with desiring,
Or of *mountain's* unique bond with
The fountains gushing forth from it that cry out of high
Things. Solitariness of *Desert* ever
Stretches out in vain,

Lonely *Monarch* of all who survey
Its wearying inclusiveness, subject to
No true attachments as a *fool's*
To his toy tool, jingling self-image, nor object of
Blunderings that it keeps ever breeding—*wife* of
Self-created strife.

Sole rondures of *day* unrolling stay
The approach of stillness, and between them and
The larger wheel of *year* appear
The lunar counterturns in cold, reflected selfhood
Of *Month*, unbound to sun but only barely out
Of phase with its rounds.

These solitaries! whether bright or
Dim, unconstellated words rain down through the
Darkness: after *youth* has burned out
His tallow truth, and *love*, which above everything must
Cling to word and body, drains, *Wisdom* remains full,
Whole, unrhymable.

Intone them then: *Breadth Circle Desert
Monarch Month Wisdom* not for whatever spell
They generate but for their mere
Inexorable syntax. The eye's movement outward
Claims its huge dominions not by kinship, nor bond
Of common ending.

THE QUESTION OF HATS

A high climax of head
Capped? A truest height crowned?
A radiance hooded?
The problem is whether——
Bareheaded in the wind
That clutches the tussocks
That thatch the rocks——whether
The spirit of the sky
Will fall about him to
Sustain him in complete
Cap, or whether those blasts
Tearing his hair have rushed
At that head as if to
Finish a creation
Interrupted——to place
There a tin cone with a
Green banner above it;
A felt gasket sealing
A top; a wool; a wire
Cage wherein eyes might perch;
A fur *schtreimel* with fleas;
A shining carrousel
Around which three monkeys
Chase the Wickety-Wa!
Repairs for a lost crown
Of light! Ach——all these hats!
One knows an Assistant
Gulliber by his whine,
A Chief Deceiver by
His whiteness, a killer
By the smell of his mind:
Away with all their hats
And hoods (which in the end

Are always to be doffed)!
Liberate all the heads!
Why, at the shrine of Saint
Bright, the hats are all piled
Up along the roadside
Like the junked wheelchairs at
All the places like Lourdes.
When it rains, let his high
Part drink; when it darkens,
Let his dome peer through grass
At its own dark mirror.
When it dawns, let him hear
Barefoot antipodes
Padding through the low leaves
At the world's other top.

ROTATION OF CROPS

Farmer John wandered among his fields
Feeling a tedium of the soil
Lifted by no pious following
Of oats by peas, then of peas by beans,
And then beans by orient barley,
Or even the peaceful fallowness
Yielding what little that peace can yield.
No dew pearled rough furrows with early
Seeds of shining along their low sills.

What could revolve there was not the sun.
Twilight kept shifting between evils
—Heaviness, then alleviation;
Only Sol smoldered with tedium
In the untenanted meads above,
There, where no other kinds of light grazed.
Below, no other kinds of light grew.
"And so, and so" groaned the Farmer John
And gazed at the vagueness of his grain.

But then after dark the night itself
Shifted her ground: cerements of turf
Flung back the rough darkness threshed away
From fire toward the stars' clear counterpane;
Hectares of millet, disgusting field
Of vetch, acres of darkened corn, were
Turning in the starlight that seeded
Them all, while the sleeping Farmer gleaned
Mindfulls from outside the mills of light.

The Head of the Bed

for Robert Penn Warren

At the mountainous border of our two countries there is a village; it stands just below a pass, but some of the older houses lie higher up along the road, overlooking more of the valley than one might think. The border has never been heavily guarded, and our countries are peaceful. Theirs lies beyond the pass; in the other valley a large village looks up toward the mountains and toward us. The border itself is marked only by an occasional sign; but then there is the Trumpeter. His clear, triadic melodies break out through the frosty air, or through the swirling mists. From below, from above, the sound is commandingly clear, and it seems to divide the air as the border divides the land. It can be heard at no fixed intervals, and yet with a regularity which we accept, but cannot calculate. No one knows whether the Trumpeter is theirs or ours.

I

Heard through lids slammed down over darkened glass,
Trees shift in their tattered sheets, tossing in
Shallow sleep underneath the snoring wind.

A dream of forests far inside such sleep
As wakeful birds perched high in a dread wood,
Brooding over torn leaves, might mutter of

Rises over the pain of a snapped twig
That ebbs and throbs not with a shore rhythm
But with the pulsings of dark groves—as if

A bird of hurting swept over hooded
Places, fled, and at intervals returned—
Clocked by the broken aspirates roaring

Along their own wind, heard within their wood,
Their own deep wood, where, fluttering, first words
Emerge, wrapped in slowly unfolding leaves.

2

Where, where, where? Where is here? Where is Herr Haar,
Tendrils lashing across the light his eyes
Open on, Joker of Awakening?

Where is where? Where the cracked suddenness wide
On that frail wall, where amber filigree
As of an egg's marble vein his pillow;

Where webby vines clinging coldly to his
White eyeball fall away to dust; where hair
Hangs across the world, here is where. And there

Is the acknowledging skull of far wall—
Two hollow, shaded windows and a smudge
Of dark mirror between. And there is here

No light. Not yet. Deep in the woods' heart, soft,
Dim leaves close up again; heat lightning rips
Pallid sheets, silent, across roughened sky.

3

Floor lamps and their shadows warmed the room where
He lay dead in bed; and then the windows
Were thrown open to admit of the night.

Exhalations of buses rose hoarsely
Over the reservoir's onyx water
Beaded about with lights, an appalling

Brooch clutching the appalling shawl of the
Dark park through whose trees no relieving wind
Blew. No zephyr sniffed the window curtains

Pushing through the stuff of outer silence
That cars coughed in; only an old great-aunt
Waited, on her nightly visitation,

Denied again by his awakened, dark
Blood, as come bubbling up bone-gathering
Trumpetings of unscheduled, sombre cocks.

4

Slanting, lean, gray rain washing the palace
Steps floods the inner court: Vashti mutters
There, dripping among her ancillaries,

Of displeasure, loss, and now a cold walk
To distant parts of the palace, gutters
Roaring with possibilities, water

Burbling the Ballade of All the Dark Queens—
Not the wet abjects, but those who yet reign
(*Where is Lilith?*) in that they could refrain—

Not Hagar sent out among the dry rocks,
But Orpah opting for hers, and Martha
Answering her own hearth and electing

The bubbling merriment of her pudding,
Reading the night-girl Lilith's name in white,
Vanishing from her windy, drying sheets.

5

Coarse breath fanning the closed air by his ear
Stirred up the swarming night-bees who had been
Honeying nearby, where faces blossomed

Out of the darkness, where creepers mingled
With long, low-lying trunks, humming among
Damp hollows, herding and gathering there,

But unheard by him undreaming, by him
Beamed in upon by the wide moon who smeared
Light here and there into dark surfaces—

Madam Cataplasma, her anointment
Vast, her own outstretched form fantastic there
Beside him, as if on awakening

A filthy myth of Lilith would lie spilled
Like darkness on the sheet of light. He rolled
Out of this bad glade and slept darkly on.

6

He felt his hand feeling another hand
Feeling his own: staring up after a
Fly's noisiness, his bony image lay

Where he was beside himself, imbedded
In the nearby, the space readied and wide
And yawning, fed up with the emptiness

Of its tents, rags of cloudy percale hung
Over bumps and hummocks. It shaded them,
He and he lying and listening while

Kicked fabric fell softly over their bones.
Sighing settles: toward what does buzzing fly?
About what does the sound of breathing dream?—

An echo fleeing down twisted halls; a
Buzzing fly rising over him and his
Like something bland and vague deserting them.

7

Down the shaded street, toward an avenue
Of light, a gleaming picture receded:
The sudden lady, tall, fair and distant

Glided slowly, and her beautiful leg
Sole but unlonely, swung walking along
Between the companionable crutches,

Flesh hand in hand with sticks. He followed them
And waited in a sunny place, and when
She halted, there were woods. Turning her head,

She smiled a bad smile, framed by a shadow
Flung from a tower somewhere. He dared not move
Toward her one leg, toward her covered places

Lest he be lost at once, staring at where
Lay, bared in the hardened moonlight, a stump
Pearly and smooth, a tuft of forest grass.

8

The Hyperboreans gathered him up
And bore him across, out of the shadows,
Into their realm of tenderness where there

Is room enough, but where there are no gaps
Between the seeding and the gathering;
Nor wintering, in which recovering

Desire grows in its caves, nor the buzz
Of endless August, golden, deified:
No need for these. In that bland land he lay—

Envisioning frost and fallen silver,
Half hearing the cricket in the parching
Oat-straw, feeling tears from his weeping brow,

Dreaming of intervals lost—stretched out on
Wastes not of snow, nor sand, nor cloud, he tossed,
And knew not why, in that undying noon.

9

Leaving that unfair, seasonless land was
More than a traverse of uneasiness;
More than an antlike file over glacial

Sheets and then, at last, across the fold of
Pass, pausing above a final valley
Shining in a new light, and shivering

At the approach of strange, dark guards; more than
Their distrust, and their icy moustaches
Masking frowns at our tokens of passage

(He held a light bulb, heavy in his right
Pocket, and they, red stones in their left ones)
More than making one's way; and returning

Over a way not yet gone over, hurt
Like first smashings of light, shrunk to a lamp
Shaded, grim, sun-colored at four AM.

Beyond the cold, blue mountain and beyond
That, we shall wander on the pale hills when
Shadows give over bending along the

Slopes, and the silent midday light, unchanged
For hours and days, is pierced only by our
Two moving specks, only by the cricket's

Warm humming. Then, what we hear becoming
What we see, the gray; the wind enclosing;
The poplars' breath; the sad, waiting chambers.

Will there have been room? There will have been room
To come upon the end of summer where
Clustered, blue grapes hang in a shattered bell,

Or there, in a far, distant field, a swarm
Of bees in a helmet, metal yielding
Honey, balmy drops glistening on bronze.

II

Half his days he had passed in the shadow
Of the earth: not the cold, grassy shade cast
By a pale of cypresses, by pines spread

More softly across stony hilltops; not
Warm, gray veiling of sunlight that blotted
Up his own moving shadow on the ground;

But the dark cloak of substance beyond mass,
Though heavy, flung with diurnal panache
Over his heavier head, weighed it down.

Way down at the bottom of a shaft sunk
Through the grass of sleep to deep stone he lay,
Draped in the shade cast inward by the place

All outward shadows fall upon, and on
His tongue an emerald glittered, unseen,
A green stone colder in the mouth than glass.

When, as if late some night of festival
The skies open, do the insides of stars
Turn slowly out? At midnight, once, he finds

Himself looking up a familiar
Street and being shown a way of water:
Bordering the calm, unsubsided flood,

Gray frame houses with darkened roofs intact,
Minding the sky of paler gray; along
The surface of gray water, the tracing

Eye's anxious questions—only these have moved.
And save where—by a window giving on
His sunken yard—someone blind makes wordless

Music while his three graceless daughters wait
In the shadows for evening, all is gray
Silence, save for his resolved organ chords.

13

He awoke. Low in the sky in August
Blown clear by a cold wind, thinned-out clusters
Of distant stars whistling through darkness struck

Out at a momentary Jupiter
Passing at night, bright visitor, among
The passages of his twinkling bazaars.

And saw strung in the Scorpion a jewel
Of unmarred garnet, the old, the reddened
But not with shed blood, nor with ripening.

And saw and read by the diamonded Harp,
By crossbow Swan aimed along the pale stream
Southward, by all the miles of undialled light,

By the mark missed, by the unstinging tail,
The moment that was: the time of this dark
Light beyond, that seemed to be light above.

14

Grayish flakes like clay are falling as if
Of the sky falling at last on Chicken
Big, now grown huge and old, examining

The falling daylight from her crowded house,
The plausible, settled-for gray, dropping
Out of its cloudy, indeterminate

Swirl, its pale precipitate vanishing
At the full bottom of its fall, too light
To have swerved, too general to pile up,

These flakes of day, in a reaction
As if of flakes of, say, fictions taking
Place *in vitro*, trembling as the flask shakes—

In vivo then? behind this mottled glass
The awakener hears the greasy rain
Collapse on unglistening streets below.

15

The bright moon offends him: he plucks it out;
He opens all the seals of touch; he hears
The whirlwinds of his breathing; then it comes:

A last waking to a trumpet of light
From warm lamps turns him over gravely toward
Her long, bare figure, Lady Evening,

Who, while he lay unwaking, rearranged
Oddments of day on a dressing table,
Lowered gentle blinds, letting the night dawn,

And thought of their sole parting, the breaking
Of day; his journeys into day's mock night;
His sojourn with lilting Miss Noctae, witch

Of windless darknesses; his presiding
Eye, and his slowly unwinding heart;
Then lay beside him as the lamps burned on.

PART TWO

A LATE HARVEST

The wordy winds have
Fled into the dark
Curtains of distant
Heat, leaving us these
Soundless ones, earnest
But breezy withal,
Gatherers of our
Sweat, gleaning along
Shining fields of our
Chilled whiteness in the
Mock moon of streetlight
That steals in to feel
For wall, ceiling and
Bed with another
Kind of silence from
Theirs, the taciturn
Reclaiming a dew
Of borrowed silver.

THE MUSE IN THE MONKEY TOWER
(Via dei Portoghesi)

for James Wright

American girl, within
Your room up in the tower
Above darkening houses
That squat along darkened streets,
Come to your window or his,
Because it eyes his wider
One which frames it in sunset—

Peer like a kind of day out
Of one region into all
Others, lighting up even
The farrowing street at noon
With what comes out of the dark.
Now while all the visible
Angels rest their stone trumpets

In the hot light, Olive, for
Instance, recollects her brood
Of cloudy doves, passengers
For ages beyond our own:
Ripe-eyed, she keeps all the rest,
But what will come will never
Come of the peaceable hours;

Thus Myrtle, perhaps, our old
Dear substrate, mincing to what
One might dare call her casement,
Would beam admittance to her
Shady bed and a hot fuck
Under the *tramontana*:
What was to come would not cool;

52

And even Laura, cooler
Than the darkest greens of her
Northwest, waiting for evening
As long as if for ever,
Aureate hair catching a
Brightness from beyond her own,
Leaping from the wider day:

No, that lady will not be
Whistled for, and the comic
Lauro from downstairs, poking
Out of his hole in the wall
Shouting for Massimo, comes
Justly rebuking the wrong
Call directed far too high.

You there who are left, Judith
Or Joan or whoever dwells
In the magic tower now,
Gaze across with eyes of sky
Into the shadowed room where
He waits for what will come and
Seize him as if with your light.

KLEINES MÄRCHEN

After the frosty sunup
Crystals of grass lay scattered
Wide across unmined green, till
Broken noon burned momently
In that brief space of brightness
When glass, the sad glass, is gold.

But ah, the race of the cold
Shade fast across our pastures!

Frozen grass tinkled against
Sides of a long well; again
Transparencies unclothed in
A revel of clarity,
Soft though the shadows were of
Moon; the errant of borrowed
Wings could read by his gibbous
Shield the unbottomed pits in
Dark eyes, in silver grass the
Snake, the Gorgon in the gold.

TWO ROMANTIC TRANSFORMATIONS

I

REJOICING IN AUGUST

Are you not weary, enchanted days?
Let flat and darkening August green
Tell no more of the ardent ways

Of sanguine March, and mighty Mays
And northeastern April come between:
Are you not weary, enchanted days?

The false gold in the ripening maize
Will feed no seasons of the lean:
Tell no more of the ardent ways

Its head-high labyrinth betrays,
Serving the son of the raining Queen.
Are you not weary, enchanted days?

Goldenrod's brutal yellow flays
Roadside grasses; the greens they mean
Tell no more of the ardent ways.

An early-lengthening shadow strays
Over a lawn toward woods unseen.
Are you not weary? Enchanted days
Tell no more of the ardent ways.

A SEASON IN HELLAS

You know a region higher than these crags?
A painted castle flying silly flags
Imprisons a spoiled princess, robed in fur,
Daily awaiting a dark torturer.
You know the place? O there, O there,
On fire, O my destroyer, we shall fare!

You know the valley where a thinning stream
Reflects no hopeful spires, no peaks of dream?
A ruined roadway winds down from the pass
Toward sullen sheep, gray in the withering grass.
You know the place? O there, O there,
At dawn, O my deserter, I shall stare!

You know the bed in a long-windowed room?
Night-colored curtains stir, black roses bloom;
Where moonlit harpstrings glitter like a crown
My silvery double enters and lies down.
You know the place? O there, O there,
O my lost self, we both dissolve in air!

Something About It

WHO IT WAS

Expelled naked into life,
Gathered naked out of it
(*O, save for the nakedness,
Were leaving like arriving!*),
It gave some indications
Of being like us in this.

ITS CAT

Had no fur,
But with pink
Musclings
Beneath its
Shiny pink
Skin, trembled
With the loose
Awareness
That meat might
Have if life
Escaped its
Jail of form;

Had no purr
Nor high whine
Of query,
But a sound
Of sobbing
Would come from
Wherever
It lay down;

Moved without
Feeling how
Or even
That it moved,
Table top
Barely known
To paw pad——
No whole, but
Parts dragging
Other parts.

The love It
Showed the cat?
——I shall not
Violate
A private
Matter just
As well hedged
About with
Our disgust.

ITS LUNCH

On the shining china, white and gold,
    A cold toad
Graced with pieces of lettuces, and
Unless eaten at once, somewhere past
Chambers of mauve and peacock, behind
The strings of candied stanzas, in a
    White tiled room,
A child will go on being tortured.

AT ITS DESK

Doctor Bergab, as It was known
In the office, gazed through the glum
Frame at the slum, at a distant
Inch of bridge, and the power plant
Humming, streaked with gray and green, in
A swinging pot near the ceiling:
The fruit thereof a kind of light,
It filled part of the room with its
Life, the Doctor filled the rest with
Death, all his dim volumes dumbly
Shouldered each other into the
Space remaining and doves shuddered
Outside on the narrow black ledge.

ITS NATURE STUDY

Too light to be called
A burden, inert,
The gray grasshopper
In his pocket stirred
Not, nor would it leap
Among the bedsheets
From which then Doctor
Bergab concluded
That the wish to wish
To wish to cavort
Had failed, and he searched
The half-grayish folds
Of the sheets for some
Tokens of this loss,
While the afternoon
Light in which he looked
Kept on failing too.

SICK IN BED

When ill, they gave It white
Of egg, aspics of no
Color but of certain
Venom, and snow water
Melted from the lower
Hills of sheet, running down
Unseen creases of stream
Into a kidney-shaped
Basin, white-enamelled,
On the shadowed floor, and
As they gathered for It
These distillates of blanc,
Its face lay gathering
Darkness of its own, in
The gathering darkness,
In the harvesting night.

ALMOST CLOSING TIME

Doctor Bergab twirled
The globe that was not the world.
The blur of Asia
Was the color of orange
And of dust, the thin
Layer of pale seas pasted
On the worldliness
Of mere ball kept returning
In a matter of
Seconds——the diurnal prime
Spun its tired spin
A thousand times more slowly
And more fast: staring,
Later, out at the sliding
By of evening sky
Over his shoulder, Miss Slot,
The secretary
His finger was inside of
Sounding narrow deeps
Awhirl within, never moved.
She was not the world,
And ball, office, window, girl
And sliding Doctor
Spun on borrowed centers not
Their own, and barely
Afire even with pallor.

JOE'S PLACE

Convivial darkness
    Where the gulping
Of vibes and the bass grunts
    Thickened the air:
It went there once only
    For the music.
All the others took It
    For a shadow,
Never minding what form
    Passed among them.
They were drinking a kind
    Of black whiskey.

ITS CHILDREN

It lay dreaming in the heat of Manhattan
    That its young daughter was dead,
The while she dreamed at the end of Long Island
    That she would die the next day.
Struck by light, those films of dreaming were exposed,
    But in the hot glare of noon
The day's pages fluttered and all their boring
    Inscriptions squinted back
At their reader: *Dry Cleaning* parched in the sun,
    Flowers by Wire shimmered
Among the names of all the sufficiencies,
    Lunch itself kept warm. But then
The hot glare of evening retuned all the air
    Into a homelier mode,
It sat gazing through the heat of Manhattan
    Not at that heat, but beyond
At Its own dim pages, from which gray words dripped
    Not unlike tears, or dried to
Unsuspicious stains, ghosts of ghosts of scribbles
    Not even boring, unfelt
In the unhaunted dark of a night It would,
    At best, know the thickness of.

MOUNT BLANK

Accessible by reasonably good roads most of the year; pass
open from the North, July & August. At 1973m. a rest-
house, from which one can walk, or ride by cable car, to the
western summit. The eastern face should not be attempted
without a guide.

for David Kalstone

——Until, the next morning in the sun, there
It was, framed in the window, looking like
The intense pictures of itself, which all
The night before while the ravening black
Swallowed the hills, engorged the dim vales, sucked
Up starlight through holes in the pines, and coughed
At the half-latched gate, all the night before
He lay awake, trying to remember:
Snowy veils of spume blown across the gorge;
A view shot upward dizzyingly while
The unseen ravine somehow made itself
Known, out of the picture; even the mere
Gorgeousness of depth, rock and height had dimmed.
His cold remembrances raved in the dark,
Houring after images. Midnight
Was no minimum, though: no skier whizzed
Past its momentary flatness, down one
Half parabolic dream of slope and up
Its opposite. The deadly hours which
Followed neither sank nor rose toward the day,
But merely stretched. The pictures were all wrong,
Those which came. They were pictures of pictures,
Or views of noise: postcards of roaring, as
Of mighty waters from the top of Mount
Throwdown; illuminations of the blasts
Hammering the clear tops of Mount Windows.
Or else they mirrored certain infamous
Peaks, quite as if to lead him by the head

To some mad eminence—say, the summit
Of Nayvel, to howl a loud howl like, "Down,
Be thou my Up" Or else they reflected
The ludicrous Snifflehorn rising from
His flat face on the plain bed, pictures far
Too close to themselves, and too close to him.

No, there were to be no comparisons—
Nor of the splendid reals of the morning
With night's thin images, nor of the blaze
Of day with what lay banked in a black stove,
Nor of the pictured with the picturing.
For he awoke to a deluge of light,
And, rising far beyond that light in which
His eyesight gleamed, the old and the famous
Peak, preposterous—that was what he faced.
And if it had been cut out of cardboard,
Cardboard would serve. It always had: inside
Contours part jagged, part caressingly
Smooth—for even children were trained to trace
Its silhouette that they might come to know
It—there was only the unmarked flatness
Of surface fused to its depth. What he saw
Was not a picture of his seeing, nor
An image of his dimmest sleep. And, say,
That there was no cardboard (or, if there were,
A little azure hat for the mountain,
Doing no harm), say that the crookedness
Of its high tower was a beckoning,
And that it was a place to get to—still,
Cardboard is as cardboard does: biting out
Its part of the available blue and
Masking some gummier construction taped
Behind it, emptiness and passe-partout.

And yet the vision of it hung there seemed
A vision as of something rounded, cut
Into by the wild blades of icy air,
Scooped and shaped if only by its shadows,
Troughed by a glacier and likely as not
Hacked out with caves and rock-studded across
An unseen face. And he knew a cold wind,
Then. It brought with it, as it might carry
A distant shouting among its own yells,
A blast of glimpsing from afar, a speck
Of mountaineer against the blue, plunging
Slowly from the far summit. Then the wind
Died. Frost on the glass outside gleamed under
The mounting sun, the cold snowfields stretching
Between his crying eye and that height, the
Fell beacon, gray, unsurmounted with light.

OFFICER'S QUARTERS

This room is lit by winter

And this stove, giving heat and keeping what light it has within it,

Is yet doing an act of light, even to the corner of the room

Where Captain Consciousness sits at the bare table, writing by the light of his own hand

Outside in the northern sky, above the frozen canal, dark specks of duck

Undiscernible as bird, but flying away:

Inside, the bright images and hard-edged, in the warmth, the radiance.

REMEMBERING THE FOUNTAIN

for Daryl Hine

Dry Apollo: His bright butterflies silently
    Flutter among the gray greens; motionless
Lizards ablaze with black and olive, striped with darts
    Of ochre, or spotted with everything,
Lounge on pocked steps. Carved not of the god's regular
    Marble—aflash even in ruin with
Something of his sunlight—their columns were flung up
    From the unruly rocks dashed all about
Among the pale daisies and hard, unfruitful weeds.
    They support only the unbearable
Blue of sky not, at this height, a true measure of
    The faraway: distant thoughts of water,
Of silent coasts, unimaginable islands—
    These mark where wideness is under the sun.
And there the fond, pictorial eye's greater reach
    Off southwestward frames a shadowless peak,
Where even the high travellers, poking about
    Among those wolf-grey forms would shed no shade.
And now our eye is cast back at our stony feet.
    What had been done here was done in green wood:
What do we do here now in the dry? —Remember:
    Back up toward the north-northeast, at the green
Foot of a holy mountain, old water, deep, clear
    And cold, had something to say of sunlight;
His touches of gold unwedded to her whispers
    Of frosty stream, but wet, with caressing
Amusing surfaces, and with reading clear depths.
    Not so with those three who bend over the
Fountain now: unquickened, the god who lies entombed
    In the noon sunshine; and no legacy
Of his, the almost-enduring nymphs whose voices
    Drown the rock talk and water murmuring

Deep below their discourse. Significances splash
   Up to him, standing nearby, whose they are—
The Rememberer, unknowing yet of the dry
   Heights that wait southward, and above no sea.

AFTER CALLIMACHUS

Half my soul still breathes;
Half, breathless, flutters
About in the dark
In love or running
Wild among others,
Gone over the hill.
Deserters get shot:
Help me find her; she
Is out there somewhere
Now, one of those flakes
Of white on the waves
Which play with her as
With my straining eyes.

THE HIDDEN ONES

A panic in woods—when a bewildered
Buck in the maddened moon-color of stumps
In a dry, burnt-out glade smashed the deadened
Timber all about—clutched the listener.
But no wet goat-horns hid among the dark,
Acknowledging, sacred branches: only
In the wild surge of panic's name, One kept
His own festivals yet, while for the still
Glistener on the dewy lawn, the broad
Speech of turf was empty. They who wait, wait

Behind the hoardings of ramshackle words:
Mother Golden in the cereal field,
Burnishing the grain and dross, breathing rough
Aspirations amongst dancing straws;
A Deus in the graciousness of day,
Drunk with skyeyness, who will plummet from
One high-burning spacement to another
Bearing our gains and losses, now tracing
Our flames in His, now building the basement
Below us on which our frail place still rests.

And what in water? Undinal flanks glide
And sink below themselves toward where under
Them all sits Father Form: all the daughters
In trains of tears and raindrops are his, who
Shapes their uncertain substance, their dolphin
Flashing of smile, farewell waves, sickening
Quick-sunken troughs, and raging sheets of spray
—And all with unending long arms for him
Who thinks to swim among his mother's deep
Lost fields, or to hang in their churning sky.

Even the rare walker finds in warning
Splashes of faltering, unreal light (the
Dapplings blown up to smears on film, evil
Twilights unabraded yet by streetlamps)
Their breath: the alarming ring surrounding
Lamplight itself with no glory but fear
Of pressures of the dark, is made of dance
—Of their dance, who will not stay hidden now
That an unwintered heart springs up toward them
With trembling hands made of the eye's last glance.

LEAVING DELOS

Wandering star of the heaven-colored
Sea; bright apple of her islands: I stand
Leaden-eyed in the new darkness before
An eidolon fading along thy dead
Receding shore, guarded by no buried
Head of Bran or brass chanting time is, was,
And is past. Only the rising wind sings,
Discordant, high up in the steel rigging.

A DESCRIPTION OF THE CELEBRATED STATUE
OF THE STORYTELLER AT IOANNAPOLIS

for William Bailey

Robed in a flowing of his own bronze,
He sits discoursing

Not to grouped listeners
Sitting with hands clasped about one knee

Looking up at the raised, teaching finger,
The reaching fiction pointing inward;

Not to the trees nor, among them,
The big-eyed, witnessing beasts;

Nor indeed to that which is not bronze,
Which is not silent, in the busy stoa across from him;

—But to an attendant gathering of his Stories,
Come to pay homage to their master.

Here is The Girl in the Ball, here the Sorrowful
Ferryman, and behind him, the Missing Bear;

Here's William, from The Story of William,
And, flopping mysteriously about, The Seven Enchanted
    Tuna.

Is he telling them the story of How They Were Told?
It is hard to be sure;

And we, who would be most grateful to meet,
On a hot, country road weaving through fields,

A little parade of our own fictions, say
The flaming tuba and the lion hand in hand—

Or who might be vouchsafed perhaps once
Through a door we carelessly opened

The nude girl looking neither at us
Nor at her choir of white and brown eggs on a table top—

We must learn thus
Of the masters of tale and of bronze.

In any event, see how appropriate a commendation the
    statue performs!
See how the artist has handled William's hair!

A MINOR LATE ALEXANDRIAN: ON JEALOUSY

We, the followers, are all as women,

I am an irascible rib,

It is not that we gang about the Lady with the Mirror, asking her to choose, looking anxiously not at her face but at those of our fellows, marking the falling of even a bit of radiance there;

But that we are like Fatima, Eglantine, Helga, Edna, Varvara Ivanovna and Sadie,

Among others,

Mooning among grapes, playing with each other's necks and bellies in idleness.

Who will be chosen for tonight?

Who will go to him, gowned in purple, jewelled in starlight,

To where he awaits our returnings

In his state of earth?

THE PROBLEM OF PAIN

Love is not a feeling. Love, unlike pain, is put to the test.
One does not say:
"That was not a true pain because it passed away so quickly."
— Wittgenstein

The problem of pain was that there was no problem.

On the torn page there were parts of a diagram, but the proof, the proof had not been ripped.

Like a madman leaning on the loudest bell-button, the Toothacher, behind the clouds outside, pressed neither in stupor nor in rage;

But the drilling bell never diffused into the dark air of silence.

The particle clinging to my eyeball remained an intruder; his visit could fructify in no gleaming pearl.

Spasms assaulted out of the dark of back: below that plain over which we have no eyes to gaze, they could have been hiding anywhere.

The flash of burning was soundless; its moment of waiting, dark; but its echo of hurt, crescendo, silenced the scoffers, the disbelieving tourists who stood at the edge of the gorge.

And the lunatic Toothacher again, after some years. We had moved to another city: he should not have known our address.

And his noise continued to remind us of nothing.

They all sounded, these penetrations, like nothing but themselves.

The one they called, half-fondly, *cramp* has a real name that rhymes with no word in any known language,

But which the calf of a leg roars out, wrenched in a sea of bedsheets.

Not like the twilight of fever,

Flooding the inner jungles with a lulling music: Wagnerian, or
whitening river water, or the remembering click of wheels on
rails—

Not like the shades of sorrow a kind hand drew over the afternoon
sun, down the sickroom windows, softening the edges of things
that would otherwise blur—

Nor the warming ache of strain.

Nor weariness, the final weariness shedding its wisdom over recum-
bent forms, long and lumpy beneath the blankets' shroud.

Examples

for I. A. Richards

DESCARTES' WAX

Ah yes, the wax: this piece just now unhived, now in my hand—

Honey-smelling yet, that honey yet flower-smelling, those flowers

(Say, they are purple clover, outgrowing the white)

Still remembering their houses of grass, whose green breathings

Themselves lead back into redolence, in eternal regress,

Stirred by the mind's winds; while in its house of silence,

This wax, tawnier than the honey, shines with a noble yellow,

Lion-color, golden as a beast from which strength is plucked,

A hardened blob: warmth will make it give, warmth of the near
candle's glowing mind

Lump of cerebrum: my thumbnail lines it into two lobes which
caresses will spread

Or curl

And then, and then anything

A waning of sameness: but from where—

Hoard of forms hidden in a high mountain cave? the sky's inexhaustible grayblue Morpheum?—

Will it take shape?

RUSSELL'S MONARCH

"The present king of France is bald";

For some years he has gone without the fiction of false hair,

Fringed with a slipped, half-glory of white, while a corollary gleam

Shines from his pate in the bright light, above a land of green,

As he stands for a moment, ivory orb and cue in either hand,

In the grand billiard-room at Monterreur,

Still suggesting some of his earlier pictures: as on the east terrace back
   at Montraison

In the clear light that spoke silently of betrayals, he stood watching,

First the light itself and then, distantly, welcoming clouds.

And he sighed for the truth.

Or as in state of some kind, with much plum-colored velvet swagged
   behind him,

The heavy, dripping sleeve of an abstract arm whose hand may be
   pointing somewhere,

Or keeping something out of sight.

But if one is mistaken about him, finds out he has crowned non-
   entity with the pinchbeck of language,

Elevating him who could not even be considered a pretender,

Then say, rather "The present king of France" is bald, is too crude
   an instance;

For the blunders by which we climb, those mistakes our handholds

Are less stark than the rocks we seek to rise above,

And these: the fullness and the curl of wigs, moving above a sea of
   shoulders,

Or reposing broodily on their wooden eggs at night—

Are our additions to what is given, our patches for what is always
being taken away.

TAKING THE CASE OF THE DONKEYS (*Austin*)

Spare philosophers in a bright field stand shooting at donkeys

Across the cold distance of rocky ground on which they are not

Toward pasture, and the gray, earnest ones grazing there,

One of whom finally drops, hit by accident,

Another, by mistake; but both by an unrelenting intent that they
serve not as beasts of burden,

But, winged with the Exemplary, as creatures of the mind's flight.

The philosophers may not love them—their deaths are so ridicu-
lous!—

But that would be because the philosophers are exemplary as well;

Dropping their rifles to the misty ground, and slowly merging with
its colors,

They amble toward the melted beasts and ride them solemnly

Out of our sight.

MOORE'S BEASTS

"Tame tigers growl"

Or not, as the case may be;

But some tame tigers who do not exist are ever silent of throat,

Just as they are never narrowed of eye.

Silence of paw is something else: I have been brushed by the passage
    of fiery fur

And heard soft padfall, like the slopping of something damp in the
    long hallway;

I have heard the rip and then the shredding of stretched canvas

As, patiently standing, one paw against the golden foliage of frame,

One of them came to know, after weeks of contemplation,

That a landscape of dim forests must, in fact, go.

An ounce of tears watered the carpet and his face.

I have heard them lying half asleep along the hard terraces, their
    guarded breathing.

But mostly these children of fear are seen and not heard,

Passing across open doors, slow huge heads turning dark corners,

Looking back down corridors as if—and what can one make of the
    silences of our beasts?—

Regretful: unhurried, but surely regretful.

$7 + 5 = 12$ (*Kant*)

I think I see why this one: two primes aimed at the all but inevitable
   composite

—The one which should, had we two subsidiary thumbs, have been
   our numberer,

A reasonable base for those airy towers untopped, paling into distances—

But, out of some gentleness, not stepped crudely upward,

Five and seven and then their sum—as if climbing were all that
   vertical scales were for—

Instead more warmly abstract: dipping in order to rise, but barely
   whispering of that,

Nor of mystery taken and pent up in hand.

Hand in hand, their *tableau vivant* never over,

They yet bow and smile, asserting a truth radiant even in daylight,

Like what lay somewhere between the given and the found,

Always golden and unspeakably glittering down in the cellars.

BURNING LEAVES

In Memory of Mark Van Doren

They tended a cold November fire in a field
   And watched. There was nothing to say. There were
The duodecimos of summer being burned,
   Old, damaged greenbacks consumed, to give way
Not soon but soon enough to a new currency.
   The poem of burning needed no title.
And if one muttered, "How hungry fire is" and if
   The other took the mild reminder for
A teaching, it was not drawn from any teaching
   Of the leaves, burning in the wind, imbued
In their reddish or tan pallor with a touch of
   Consummation. For there was no hunger
Of fire like that of light, frail skeletons of leaf
   Famishing for altitude now that so
Little was left. But rather, as they raked the
   Gray ashes with their gaze, uncovering
Here and there protesting tongues of flame and under
   Everything the hot, silent ember heart,
Steadfast, rather were their decipherings of fire.
   They were like the smallest girl in a group
Of four who stares at the yet unlit pyramid
   Of autumn leaves the others still heap up
As if at present flame, and like them unaware
   That a paling sequence of poplars shrinks
And fades into the dark ground in the cold of a
   Perfectly painted twilight behind them.

What, then, of the readings of leaves? Barren or green,
   Their brief flights are not theirs, but of the winds.
A careless girl in a rocky cave leaves her door
   Aflap in the gale: her journal's pages

Scatter and lie piecemeal; their only messages
        Are of their own dispersal, and the stray
Albumblatt someone pressed and framed, while legible
        Is trivial. Nor is one ever to
Come upon a huge form seated in a dark glade
        Turning over leaves of leaf, pages in
The Book of Leaves——to come upon him and perhaps
        To read in the tremblings of his hidden
Lips, and in the rustling of his beard, the very
        First versions, the earliest folios.
Thus for the two in Northern Connecticut who
        Watched the slow burning of the summer's bones
There was mere meditation: their faces opaque
        With thought, smoked with remembrances, they stood
Attending rising ghosts——but only of the leaves,
        Which, yearning to rise, finally can go up
Only in smoke. Naturalists, they eyed the flecks
        Of ash and gasps of spark. Pastoralists
Of old song, they brooded over where burning went,
        While above them the flakes of morning mist,
Invisibly radiant with information,
        Dispersed, clouded with the disturbances
Of smoke that they made and stood watching being made
        In a dying bonfire of deadened leaves.
Americanists of the air, they inhaled there
        The difficulties of dissolution,
And heard breathing the impatient signifiers——
        Consuming heat, the eaten leaves, and food
For thought as smoke becomes part of the sky——pressing
        For recognition. Far away, it goes
Without saying, there lay, under a clear sky whose
        Blue remained rinsed of all perplexities,
Some grey stone house by an unreflecting, chilled lake
        Ringed about southward by the laughing Alps.

UNDER AQUARIUS

for W. H. Auden on his 65th Birthday

Strained and worn, the winter sunlight refuses our windows'
    Invitations and waits hovering, under the shade
Afternoon still distributes; this is the moment before what
    Warm renewals there are light up the lengthening days—
Promises rather than cold regrets, a time when familiar,
    Craggy formations of rock, looking as if they were built
Up through the course of the years, not undergoing erosion,
    Come to count for more. Obsolete cadences, too—
And if these lines should fall with less mechanical footsteps
    Down the corridor's dark stretch to the end of the hall,
Yet, the longer ones yours, the shorter ones ours, they may manage
    To serve an occasion of love, gratitude, blessings and praise.

Something, at this time of year, demands a more measured cadence,
    Backs a little bit more straightened than ones we would trust:
Outside the door, in the street, the high, millenarian voices,
    Hailing the spring's delay, solemn, unserious, rise
Over the din of their feasting. Languid and unregimental,
    Hand in hand but, alas, thereby thus somehow in step,
Young people drift in the square, the evening's readying early
    Still, and the quiet shade daubing the pavements with dim
Colors of doubt, and of colder shadows awaiting their moment.
    Distant curfews wait wanly on circling winds.
Here as if light were in disrepute, now that darkness is falling,
    Some of the sadder ones huddle along the arcades,
Glaring at lamps that begin to twinkle out of our windows,
    Staring upward instead, looking for some kind of sign,
Eyes finally lighting upon the tired zodiacal emblem
    Rising, penultimate now, over the nights of our years.
Back under other signs, as chattering schoolboys, we revelled
    Hopefully on the ground your way of speaking prepared

(Froh empfanden wir uns auf klassischem Boden begeistert):
    Only our sense of sound first was awakened, and then,
Echoing through the open halls that we quarried to hide in,
    Faintly, the sound of sense: trustworthiness of a voice
Carrying over an ocean; if, like a clever young uncle,
    Helping us over the few gurus we'd ferreted out
Back at the end of the forties, then like a wise old aunt who
    Knew much more than the ropes, holding our hands in the
    dusk,
Pointing across the fields at other old candlelit houses,
    (Then they only looked strange) where a few guardians sat:
Half-silent Wittgenstein, who listened to all the retreating
    Hoofbeats of a remark, trying to follow it home;
Hunchback Lichtenberg, hanging over his puddle of language,
    Glimpsing the mirrored sky crowning his unimproved shade;
Deep Sarastro's priest, assessing Tamino's prognosis
    (*"Er ist ein Prinz,"* he said; *"Er ist ein Mensch,"* he was told)
Guarding a region of beauty where the loftiest pitches
    Resonate to the bad, keeping the basest of notes
Thoroughly good, where the golden needles of fire reflected
    Brightly from clear and cold water unravel the dark.
Ganymede, certain ancient writers remark, was this water-
    Bearer, the lovely boy stooping intently to pour
Rivers of nectar (not into an empty jug out of a full one,
    Emblem of Temperance, lip kissing the levelling lip)
Filling the bowl of space to more than mere overflowing,
    Instances of his light flooding the generous dark.
(Knaben liebt ich wohl auch, doch lieber sind mir die Mädchen:
    One might therefore have glossed differently, and the clear
Figure in outlined tunic comes to have been a soprano
    Role for some college girl, singing along to some Gluck
Only discovered last summer, moistening gently the arid
    Air of these cold, dry days.) Surely a sign hanging high
Over the rubble of nonsense built in the glimmer of starlight
    Over the disarray mental brutalities make,

Even with gentle touching, out of the loveliest landscape,
    Signifies that its own shining cannot be assigned
Values that range over more than mighty distances from us.
    Space, beyondness and light give us what meanings we need.

Even these minims of light from the setback skyscraper towers
    Glistening south of the park, winking in late-thirties films,
Wheeled in the sky you discoursed on, visions of what in a Fallen
    City's highest rise wisely acknowledge their own
Partial failure. And now the constellation that night has
    Dropped into water's chill, dark in this pool in a square,
Ringed with those crystals of light and giving them back to our
    silence,
    Rises: *Der Dichter*—if not seasonal, then all the more
Present continuingly, and *Alpha Poetae*, the brightest
    Star, the one whose name everyone always recalls,
Burns away knowingly, used to having been steered by, and glowing
    Up among us and our worlds turning in darkness around.

THE SHADES

Even the white shade could flap a black wing
As it flew and wrapped itself up, clearing
Stark panes of upper window—glassy light
Slapped his eye from a sudden firmament.
When lowered, they yielded up pale shades thrown
By an inner light past the opaque ones
They were ghosts of—the pallor of the shades
Took more toll of his waking eye than dark.
And, when drawn, black ones made the scene they framed
Squint, his large light-gathering glass ducking
Below the edge where the flat night machine
Widened the strip of wall, bed, and undressed
Flesh into a picture. And his eyes were opened,
As in blinding light the hand's shade allows.

2

"In enigma, the eyes hide their own light
Behind owl eyes of darkling glass; we find
Dull scales hardening on vision's surface
As if the unskeptical patient hoped
Somehow to chain down the beasts of wild glare,
The lions of the light. The prognosis
Is neither here nor there," the Ophthalmage
Muttered over his speculum, tapping
On the onyx tabletop, which glistened
To him unhearing, being too wild-eyed
In the way of dark spectacles which fail
To widen the openings they cover,
Two tiny bullet holes known to be too
Narrow, punched through the yielding skin of mind.

3

Feeling their dark ones to have been darkened
By the cast shadows of men full on men,
They considered how the unsounded caves
Everywhere glistened; how in the silence
Of noon, there in the square, all the lighted
Sepulchres threw no shadows about them
Nor none within; how they were all faded
Angels of each other, met outside a
Garden's walls whereon their own shadows fell,
Within which walked the clear, transparent ones,
The pair of glass, whose shadows permitted
—Everything was permitted—light outlined
By their shining-edged forms to pass back up
To clear eyes from the green, mirroring grass.

4

Black Wolfgang and gray brother Ludwig, two
Shades of cat, pussyfoot down the long hall.
All the Crayola boys in flowery
Surplices sing out of their stalls in praise
Of paling and of darkening, the light
Diastole, the heavier return,
Joy being in their dance of contrasts, life
Hanging between earthwardness and the air.
Too much of too many colors brings mud,
Touches of pale water lead to lightness,
But all gathered by the eyes' firelight,
Whose very flickerings discern themselves
To be waltzing in the masquerade of
Degree, each denser he whirling off with
Her, his frail one, darkening in his arms.

5

Never having, like orange monarchs, claimed
Bright meadows rich with daylong, green milkweed,
Or flamed amazement over a gazer,
They mottle the walls of hell; they stand in
Fives in the unreturning *traghetto*
Or wrapped up in shades of death accosting
The fancy wanderers in their tunnel;
Unprimed for darkness cast on their eyelight
Itself, these find no shadows of shades here,
No shadows more than shadows of flesh, no
Flickering images of soul, no soul—
The body's pale nightmare of mind, faded;
The mind's drop of frightened sweat at mere thought
Of body, unglistening, chilled and dried.

6

With the light ever going, they live with
No walker in the cool of the evening,
Acknowledging light under chestnut leaves
In solemn motley genuinely flecked;
Uncheckered their dale, their evening no flung
Counterpane nor dark-knitted comforter,
Even, under which they crowd with their own
Heats and lights still clutched and minded; feeling
The first chill of autumn only in sleep,
They awaken to yellow sun ducking
Low under the shades to stretch trapezoids
Over a dark floor. And they sleep unminding
The time of afternoon, nearly before
The cold fading unrolled along the grass.

KRANICH AND BACH

(A brand of piano no longer made)

Under her golden willow a golden crane
Hangs over golden water, stencilled on the
Heavy lamplit brown of the solemn upright:

Silence standing in a pool of reflection?
Or, if the brook's waters rumble darkly on,
Silence reflecting by a flow of music?

No golden harp with golden wires depends from
The vaulted branch on the shiny varnished ground,
Mirroring the ebony and ivory,

And the glint of golden from a wedding-band,
And the earnest hands of my poor father, who
With forgotten fingers played as best he could,

Muttering, or even roaring out the texts:
Erl-King strokes the boy; trout die in their now-dulled
Stream; the wan Double carries on in moonlight;

Impatience stutters on the keys; water turns
Through its rippling figures, and always the old
Man, bare amid a few tattered chords, still stands

Grinding out his music, *dyum de dum dum dum*:
"Both his feet are bare upon the frozen ground,
In his empty saucer no coin makes a sound."

Lyre-man, I would not know for years that you
Stand at the end of a journey of winter
To be followed only into its silence

As I will follow my father into his.
Dark under the closed lid, Kranich and Bach wait,
Silence standing up one-leggedly in song.

John Hollander's first book of poems, A CRACKLING OF THORNS, *was chosen by W. H. Auden as the 1958 volume in the Yale Series of Younger Poets;* MOVIE GOING AND OTHER POEMS *appeared in 1962,* VISIONS FROM THE RAMBLE *in 1965,* TYPES OF SHAPE *in 1969, and* THE NIGHT MIRROR *in 1971. He wrote a book of criticism,* THE UNTUNING OF THE SKY, *and edited both* THE LAUREL BEN JONSON *and, with Harold Bloom,* THE WIND AND THE RAIN, *an anthology of verse for young people, an anthology of contemporary poetry,* POEMS OF OUR MOMENT *and was a co-editor of* THE OXFORD ANTHOLOGY OF ENGLISH LITERATURE. *He is the editor (with Anthony Hecht) of* JIGGERY-POKERY: A COMPENDIUM OF DOUBLE DACTYLS. *Mr. Hollander attended Columbia and Indiana Universities, was a junior fellow of the Society of Fellows of Harvard University, and taught at Connecticut College and Yale. He is now Professor of English at Hunter College and the Graduate Center,* CUNY.

$7.95

"John Hollander's new poetry moves on a dazzling multitude of levels between the pre-historic past and the post-historic present, breathing new life into the quizzical artifacts of the latter so that they become true icons for today, re-arranging and charting its shapeless perspectives. A galaxy of voices from Callimachus to Cohen on the Telephone surges into a single voice that speaks with a new, witty authority: anarchically erudite, mocking, hopeful, melancholy, funny, romantic. This is Hollander's profoundest and richest work so far."

John Ashbery

JOHN HOLLANDER
TALES TOLD OF
THE FATHERS

John Hollander emerges in this book as a major figure in contemporary poetry in English. He has long been known to a literary audience as a figure of importance as poet, teacher, critic and anthologist. It seems clear that with *Tales Told of the Fathers* he will take his place as an important maker. From the playful to the profound, these poems reveal a sensibility and wit the range of which can be matched by very few of his contemporaries.

He has been properly praised by his peers. On the publication of *The Night Mirror* (1971), his last book of poems, **Harold Bloom** said, "I am moved to claim for these poems a vital place in that new Expressionistic mode that begins to sound like the poetry of the Seventies that matters, and that will survive us."

It is safe to say that the high quality of the work in this generous selection of poems written since *The Night Mirror* will consolidate the position for which that statement makes claim.